WALLACE NUTTING

Wallace Nutting

WALLACE NUTTING

LOUIS M. MAC KEIL

SAUGUS, MASSACHUSETTS
SAUGUS HISTORICAL SOCIETY, INC.
1984

SAUGUS HISTORICAL SOCIETY
BOOKLET NO. 2

Cover: One of a series of pentype silhouettes done for Nutting by Ernest John Donnelly, undoubtedly inspired by the poem, "Mary Had a Little Lamb."

The Library of Congress has cataloged the first printing of this edition as follows:

MacKeil, Louis M. (Louis Malcolm), 1900-
  Wallace Nutting / Louis M. MacKeil. — 2nd ed. —
Saugus, Mass. : Saugus Historical Society, 1984.
   47 p. : ill. ; 22 cm. — (Saugus Historical Society booklet ; no. 2)
   Bibliography : p. 44.
   ISBN 0-936363-03-7 (pbk.) : $3.50

   1. Nutting, Wallace, 1861-1941. 2. Congregational churches—
United States—Clergy—Biography. 3. Photographers—New England—
Biography. 4. Furniture workers—New England—Biography. 5. New
England—Biography. I. Title. II. Series.
CT275.N787M3 1984   709'.2'4—dc19   84-5429
                    [B]   AACR2 MARC

WALLACE NUTTING

IDLENESS SPOILS THE IDLE. His character rots. He is a human liability." So said Wallace Nutting in the chapter in his *Biography* he called "Guide Posts." This at no time could have been said of him from his youth to his death in 1941.

Wallace Nutting was born on November 17, 1861. His birthplace, Rockbottom, Massachusetts, was a village in the southern part of Stow (now called Gleasondale) near the Stow-Hudson line, and, as he quotes, "on the hill toward Marlborough." His birth was registered in Marlborough, which was six miles south. This no doubt is why many articles written about him refer to his birthplace as Marlborough. He was the son of Albion and Elizabeth Sanborn (Fifield) Nutting.

As the Civil War had begun, Albion Nutting enrolled in the Union Army on July 26, 1862, about nine months after the birth of Wallace, and was mustered in on August 18, 1862, at Camp Stanton on the eastern shore of Suntaug Lake in Lynnfield, Massachusetts, in Company A of the 39th Regiment, Massachusetts Volunteers.

It is rather interesting to me that my great-grandfather Nathan Reed of Natick, Massachusetts, also enrolled in the Union Army and was mustered in, in Company I of the 39th Regiment, at Camp Stanton on August 25, 1862, one week after Albion Nutting, and they were no doubt engaged in some of the same battles. I have often wondered if they ever met during their time of service.

Albion Nutting died at the Emory Hospital in Washington, D.C., on October 14, 1864, of dysentery, a very prevalent disease at that time among the soldiers, and is buried in the Arlington National Cemetery, Section 13, Grave 9515.

The foregoing facts refute the distorted account detailed in an article on Wallace Nutting published at the time of the bicentennial celebration at Manchester, Maine, in 1975. The article stated that "his father, Albion Nutting, volunteered for the rebel army when his young son was only a few months old."

Albion Nutting bequeathed the bible he carried during his army service to Wallace, in which he inscribed: "Poolesville, Md., Christmas 1862. This

5

bible I give to my baby boy Wallace. May it teach him to follow the great Captain of our Salvation." I have never seen any account of what became of it.

After the death of his father, Wallace's mother and his sister Edith, who was two years older than Wallace, moved to Industry, Maine, in 1865, to live with his grandparents. He spent his boyhood between Industry and Manchester, Maine, where he worked on the farm of his uncle Hubbard Fifield and attended grammar school there.

At age 11 he attended a private "High School" started by "a wonderful teacher" of his by the name of Stevens. Here he met his wrestling companion Fred Snow, who was a life-long and a "First Line Friend."

Wallace Nutting in later years did make a list of "First Line Friends," which has been unpublished to date, although available to me, not being released so as not to possibly offend friends or relatives as to Nutting's preference.

After the private "High School" he attended Augusta High, but in 1876 at age 15 he left school due to health problems. He worked for three years at various clerking jobs and spent one year in Minneapolis, Minnesota. His only sister Edith had died about this time at age 18.

In 1880 he entered Exeter Academy and attended it for three years. Unfortunately, all reference to him and his attendance there was lost in a fire in later years. He did not return to complete his fourth year, thereby not graduating.

During 1883 to 1886 he attended Harvard University and during the summers of those years he acted as hotel manager at Campobello; Nantucket; Martha's Vineyard; and Cheyenne Mountain, Colorado. He did not graduate from Harvard, but while there he became "bull dog" for the widow of Governor Elihu Washburne; that is, he slept in the house, "according to a custom of obtaining exemplary students where elderly ladies were timid."

In 1886 and 1887 he attended Hartford Theological Seminary and Union Theological Seminary of New York, but again there is no record of his graduating from either of these schools, although his name appears on a list of 23 graduates who were living fifty years later, in reference to a reunion. In the interim of attending these two schools he acted as pastor at the Congregational Church, Fryeburg, Maine.

Although there is no record that Nutting took a degree at either of the foregoing schools, he was ordained as a Congregational minister on November 14, 1889, at the Park Congregational Church in St. Paul, Minnesota.

He was pastor at the Belleville Congregational Church in Newark, New Jersey; the Park Congregational Church; and in 1891 the Plymouth Congregational Church in Seattle, Washington. While there his congregation grew so large, a new church was built. He also built a new house for himself there in 1892.

In 1893 he received the degree of Doctor of Divinity from Whitman College, Walla Walla, Washington, where he founded a scholarship in appreciation of advice given to him by "a notable clergyman." He also received the degree of Doctor of Humanities from Washington and Jefferson College, Washington, Pennsylvania, on June 8, 1935, where he gave an address of "The Quest for Beauty" at the commencement exercises.

On June 5, 1888, he married Mariet (Marietta) (Griswold) Caswell at Colrain, Massachusetts. She was the widow of Albert Caswell and eight years senior to Wallace, he being 27 years old at the time. There were no children of this marriage. So ended this branch of the Nutting family.

Mariet was born in Buckland, Massachusetts, on September 29, 1853, in the old Griswold homestead erected by her grandfather Joseph, where

Wallace Nutting built this house at 1320 University St. in Seattle in 1892 while serving as pastor at the Plymouth Congregational Church. According to the deed, he paid $1500 in gold coins for the property.

Mary Lyon taught school in the attic. Mount Holyoke College grew up as a result of the spirit of Mary Lyon.

In 1894 he received a call from the Union Congregational Church in Providence, Rhode Island, and remained there until ill health forced him to resign in 1904. He built a new house on Wentworth Ave. in 1900.

Although his hair had turned white at an early age, and vertigo prevented his preaching for some years, he did have periods of six or eight months where he supplied pulpits of well-known churches, during summers.

Marietta Griswold Nutting about the time of her marriage to Wallace Nutting.

Adventures in Picture Making

His picture taking career started in 1897, while at Providence, where he took long bicycle rides into the country on Mondays, no doubt to relax from his ministerial duties. It appeared to him that if he took along his camera the journeys would become shorter and more fruitful. He later purchased a larger camera which could only be transported in a carriage.

As he had the faculty of good composition, his pictures began to be sought for publication, and what monetary returns he received from his pictures went for more elaborate apparatus.

If the Monday was stormy, his wife suggested he try taking an interior, or as he called them, "personals" or "colonials," sometimes using models.

After he resigned his pastorate he was accused of leaving the church to make money as the revenue from the pictures was so large. Not true.

He opened a studio in New York on 23rd St. and was there a year, 1904 to 1905. He believed he could do better in the country, so he gave up this venture and purchased a farmhouse in Southbury, Connecticut, in 1905 and restored it. This place he called "Nuttinghame," and he established the business there as Wallace Nutting, Incorporated. In 1907 he established a branch studio in Toronto, Canada, but it was soon closed, not proving profitable, too expensive.

His first pictures were mostly of birches and then next the apple blossom pictures, and for six years most of his pictures, including interiors, were taken in Vermont.

A good deal of the success of his pictures was due to the use of platinum prints, or "platinotypes," printed on a platinum type paper, superior to the shiny black surface, the common method. He has been credited by many as being the first to use this method of printing and hand-coloring with water colors the pictures he produced, but this is not so as there are platinum print photographs in the Metropolitan Museum of Art dated 1897.

There were a great many printing processes but nothing equalled the old platinum process for beauty and expense. When the Great War (World War I) broke out, platinum was finally commandeered, as most of it was obtained from Russia, only a few ounces being found in America at this time.

So-called substitutes were provided and gave a good effect but could not equal the platinotype. Although he used these substitutes, Nutting felt that only time would tell if they endured. The purpose was to produce a print

"Decked as a Bride" (No. 73) One of the earliest and most popular of Nutting's apple blossom pictures, it was taken in Franklin County, Mass., in 1900. It was later selected as one of the subjects for his process prints.

without any film whatever on the surface, to effect a good black and white for coloring.

In using the platinum paper it was possible to salvage from the trimmings and settlings half the cost of the paper, which was purchased in rolls costing about twenty dollars each, and sometimes as many as five rolls would be used in a day.

After the washing process of the prints was completed, they became somewhat porous and the colors would sink in too much, and necessitated the colorist going over the work twice. To prevent this, a sizing of banana oil was carefully brushed or floated on the print to seal up the pores, and after drying, the coloring could be done. The coloring stayed on the surface and gave the picture a more effective and brighter appearance. The colors used were moist water colors by Winsor & Newton and were imported from London, England. They were of many colors and came in small porcelain pans 1-1/8 by 3/4-inches and 3/4-inches square. When coloring, the girls used a porcelain palette with five divisions for the various colors required.

Wallace Nutting had specific rules to follow and supervised the coloring when only a few girls were employed, but as the business grew and more girls were hired, he appointed a head colorist to oversee the work. She would color the print and if up to his standards he would approve it and this became the "model" used by others. This was not an "assembly line" procedure as thought by many, as each girl did her own print, one color at a time until finished.

The small prints were done in sheets of from nine to twenty pictures on a sheet, expecially the 3 by 2-inch size. Colorists were paid sixty cents a sheet for this work, with other sizes in proportion. For prints larger than 2 by 3 inches they were paid from four cents up to two dollars for the "W" size (20 by 40 inches), this being the largest he produced, usually framed unmounted.

The coloring was done in a well-lighted room, and in some cases the easels, which set on a small table, were constructed of a wood lath frame, covered with corrugated cardboard, and then covered with brown wrapping paper. The easels sloped up from front to back, and as they were light in weight they could be lifted to store unfinished prints under them at the end of the day. The brush handles, having pointed ends, were stuck in the cardboard at the corners when not in use.

Some of the girls also did the mounting and the framing of prints. It has been said that Nutting had 100 girls working for him while he was in Saugus, but this seems to be a controversial number, according to some of the "girls" who have been interviewed recently.

Wallace Nutting's colorists at Southbury, Ct. Ruth Harris Young is the second from the left.

Besides having tried studios in New York and Toronto, he had a studio in the Webb House in Wethersfield, Connecticut, a branch of his Framingham studio. This house he partially restored, but in his desire to have a studio he removed the old ovens from the kitchen to give him more room. He also had a museum in the other rooms. Nutting wrote a story of the house (not dated) and he called it "Hospitality Hall," but in his story he made no mention of the kitchen or what use he put it to.

This house is presently owned and maintained by the National Society of Colonial Dames of America, and if the name of Wallace Nutting is mentioned by anyone in a tour group, it is treated with scorn, and nothing mentioned of him at all by the hostess, no doubt due to the changing of the kitchen for his studio which he never restored back.

Also about this era he bought and restored the Cutler-Bartlett House in Newburyport, Massachusetts, and established a branch studio there, coloring pictures and displaying furniture. Here worked Miss Margaret Hennessey and her sister Elizabeth as colorists for two years. At a later date this house was sold to the Catholic Church, and the contents to a buyer of antiques, and the colorists went to Saugus to work in the old Scott Mill, where Margaret became a teacher of coloring and worked for five years.

Miss Hennessey told of an amusing incident that occurred while at Saugus. The girls were sitting on the lawn after their lunch hour, when

The only known pictures of the Saugus colorists are halftone reproductions. From the left, the known individuals are (2) Mary Cookley, (3) Dorothy Gage, (6) Ruth Boardman, and (12) Helen Roger.

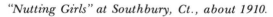

"Nutting Girls" at Southbury, Ct., about 1910.

they should have been working, and Nutting came along and asked what was going on and they replied they were on strike for more money. He told them to "stop the foolishness and get back to work," and the girls complied immediately. Nothing further was heard from this.

Miss Hennessey said "Mr. Nutting was a kind and humane man," although the girls were cautioned "no talk during working hours."

It seems Nutting was a lover of doughnuts, expecially home-made ones, and Miss Hennessey says the word got around that he was fond of doughnuts and the ladies vied with one another to make the best and at noon he was seen when outside the studio with four doughnuts, one on each of his fingers on one hand twirling them, saying, "This is my dinner." This would be topped off with hot chocolate, although he suffered greatly with indigestion.

At the age of 17 Louis Husson also worked at the Old Scott Mill in the picture department and said one day someone stole Nutting's bag of doughnuts. He also said Mr. Nutting was a "nice feller" to work for.

"Nuttingholme," Framingham Center, Mass. This was Wallace Nutting's home from 1912 until his death in 1941.

In 1912 Nutting decided to sell the farm in Southbury as well as the picture business, having a different buyer for each. The farm was sold, but the buyer for the picture business was let down by his associates and Nutting retained it.

After looking around for a week, the Nuttings were passing through Framingham Center, Massachusetts, and seeing a "For Sale" sign at a house on Vernon Street decided at once to buy, as they thought it was a good dwelling. This included a cottage on the side street, which was sold in later years.

This was the old Clark House, changed from its original style to somewhat of an Italian villa type on the outside. This home the Nuttings called "Nuttingholme." Here Nutting reestablished his picture business for the present time. Mr. and Mrs. Nutting lived out their lives here.

At Nuttingholme, due to Mrs. Nutting's efforts, a garden was created around a meandering pool, which was once a muck bed. The Nuttings called it "Little Paradise," and in this paradise, and the garden bordering their home, which supplied the flowers for Mrs. Nutting's "Floral Arrangements," over 300 pictures were taken.

These were done personally by Mrs. Nutting using antique vases, pitchers, stoneware, and baskets to hold the bouquets of selected flowers or a combination of flowers and they were photographed by Nutting. A few were titled, but all were signed or initialed "W.N."

The best of these were what Nutting called his "Deluxe" pictures, 8 by 10 inches framed close with a gold scoop-type moulding 1½ inches wide, unusual for a Nutting picture.

These pictures were often signed on the front by Wallace Nutting. I am fortunate to have three of these: "A Wild Rose Bouquet," "Zinias," and "Larkspur and Lillies." I also have ten of the glass negatives from which other of his florals were done.

At one time Del Goding of Saugus was acting as Nutting's chauffeur, and on a trip to Nutting's home in Framingham there was a long period of waiting, and Nutting told Del to help Mrs. Nutting in her garden. Del of course refused and said he was hired as a chauffeur, not a gardener, and when Nutting insisted, Del pulled out his driver's license and showed Nutting, commenting, "See here, this says 'Chauffeur'," whereupon Nutting did not press any further. It seems at that time there was a difference between a chauffeur's license and an operator's license, the first being somewhat prestigious.

The gardener and handyman for the Nuttings at Nuttingholme was John Kelly, who also worked in the picture department for Nutting at the

"Spires of Hope" (No. 1889) The spires of the First Parish Unitarian and the Plymouth Congregational Churches in Framingham Center are seen in this photograph of Nutting's garden, "Little Paradise," adjoining his home.

"A Sheffield Basket" (No. 9001) Mrs. Nutting not only did the floral arrangements for these photographs but also supplied the titles.

16

Scott Mill. He was married to Helen May Brown of Saugus, who worked as a colorist there.

In July 1975 I visited the location of Mrs. Nutting's garden at Nuttingholme and found that the "meandering pool" still existed in part, as well as some of the perennial flowers of the original garden. Of course it was greatly grown up with weeds and bushes, but the evidence of the garden and some of the steppingstones could still be found. The beech trees which appear in some of the original pictures of the garden have grown to an enormous size as if to guard the approach to the garden and pool. Pictures were taken at the time.

Some of the area has been filled in to make a parking lot for the new church building, after the old house had been demolished, but what remains of the "Little Paradise" has been made into the First Parish Garden and the "Mariet and Wallace Nutting Path," which was dedicated on October 10, 1976, as such, commemorating the 275th anniversary of the First Parish in Framingham "and could also recall and honor Mariet and Wallace Nutting, who lived on the land which the garden lies, and made it a place of great beauty."

In memory of this dedication there is a plaque on a huge rock at the area, and work will continue to increase the beauty of the garden and its surroundings.

Adventures in Writing

Wallace Nutting's adventures in writing were many and varied. He made his first trip abroad in 1904, traveling along the coast of Italy and through the Holy Land and Palestine, where he took many pictures.

He furnished seventeen of these pictures with the descriptive text for the book *The Cruise of the Eight Hundred,* dedicated to the Sunday schools of the world, published by the Christian Herald Press in 1905, and he was acknowledged as follows: "We gratefully acknowledge the contributions of original photographs from Rev. Wallace Nutting, D.D."

His literary work for magazines and periodicals started in 1899 and continued throughout his life. He wrote for *Century Magazine, Woman's World, Woman's Home Journal,* and *Outlook Magazine,* as well as many articles for *Antiques Magazine* in which he also advertised his reproductions, books, and lectures. He also contributed articles to the *Seng Book* (a furniture salesmen's book published by the Seng Co.), *The Saturday Evening Post, House Beautiful, Connoisseur Magazine,* and no doubt others not mentioned here.

In 1913 he published *Old New England Pictures,* his first real venture into publishing. This contained at least 32 of his early pictures (in some cases the pictures varied in different books as to subject and amount), and there were not many of these books published. Collectors consider it a very scarce and desirable shrine of early life in New England, in reference to the fireplaces, stairways, porch, and the interiors of old houses, their furnishings, and customs of the times.

There is also a descriptive text of each picture contained therein. In the foreword Nutting says: "The life of our fathers is worthy of more attention than it has received. This book is only a beginning and it has not come too soon, as it is already very difficult to find old houses still filled with the old life." As far as I know, there are only three of these books in existence today.

His first book on furniture was published in 1917 while he was at Saugus and was titled, *A Windsor Handbook Comprising Illustrations & Descriptions of Windsor Furniture of All Periods Including Side Chairs, Armchairs, Comb-Backs, Writing-Arm Windsors, Babies' High Backs, Babies' Low Chairs, Child's Chairs, Also Settees, Love Seats, Stools, & Tables.* This volume is also known by its cover title of *American Windsors.*

These were pictures of original pieces from 1725 to 1825, some museum owned, some owned by private homes, but mostly those owned by Wallace Nutting, as displayed in his five restored houses, and also in his home in Framingham. This handbook was published by "Wallace Nutting Incorporated, Saugus, Mass.," but some may be found with a label applied over this as being published by "Old America Company, Framingham and Boston," which came after he reestablished his business in Framingham in 1924.

It has been thought by many people that this was a book of his own reproductions. Not so, as the reproductions were shown in several catalogs.

In 1912, while at Framingham, Wallace Nutting published a catalog or book, being studies of scenes and the way of life in America and other lands, "set forth for the benefit of our friends," showing some of the reproductions of his pictures. This book was done in a light sepia color on paper made especially for this issue, and in some cases the pictures were titled and had a descriptive commentary, and they were numbered with a letter preceding the number; the letter designated size, and the number designated the title as found in the numerical and alphabetical indexes. The numbers ran from 1 to 2905, but not consecutively, as a great many numbers were omitted, due no doubt to Nutting's opinion of the subject's importance. It was somewhat of a lavish book and the edition remained as the standard, and his new work was shown in occasional supplements, such as *Wallace Nutting Pictures Expansible Catalog* of 1915 and 1917. This book of 1912 was usually only loaned to the recipient unless otherwise stated on the inside cover.

In 1921 he published the first edition of *Furniture of the Pilgrim Century*. This was done by Marshall Jones Company, Boston, publishers, and was generally confined to furniture of 1620 to 1720, and also included colonial utensils and hardware. It was dedicated to his friend Henry W. Erving of Hartford, Connecticut, who no doubt was also an antiquarian, as Nutting says, "who early discerned that the strength and beauty of Pilgrim furniture was an expression of character." Many of Erving's antiques are shown in this volume. This was followed in 1924 by his "Completely Revised and Greatly Enlarged" edition of *Furniture of the Pilgrim Century,* also dedicated to Erving.

This contained deletions of first edition pieces of doubtful American origin and makes corrections on others. Greater attention was paid to dimensions, dates, and the woods used, and the matter of ownership was brought up to date as far as known. It also contained sketches of parts of furniture as well as a very detailed description of the pieces shown and additional ironwork.

Both the first and revised editions contained many pictures of room interiors of various houses, but this writing will center on those taken in the Iron Works House at the Saugus Iron Works, as shown in the revised edition and identified as plate numbers. In the description below, the plates are also identified by Nutting's photograph numbers. In general, he numbered photographs taken in the Iron Works House in the 9300 series.

The first Saugus interior is plate number 268, "17th Century Parlor," with a commentary on page 269. This Nutting titled "Chintz and Chat" (number 9311); this also appeared in the first edition. Plate number 299, "A 17th Century Room," is again the parlor looking toward the porch, with a commentary on page 287: "Exhibits a room with stately chairs and a huge fireplace. . . ." Although no title or number could be found for this picture, it is assumed it is "Matching Chintz" (9347), also in the first edition.

Plate number 608-611, "Slender Post Bed," was taken in the kitchen chamber; the Nutting title is presumed to be "A Dowry Chest" (9363), with a commentary on page 432, also in the first edition. Continuing on, plate number 620-624, "Low Double Arched Head Bed and Trundle Bed," shows a picture of the parlor chamber with a a commentary on page 442. The Nutting title is "A Gran'ma and Gran'pa Bed" (9331). It also appeared in the first edition.

Plate number 673-674, "Trestle Bed with Spindles, Early 17th Century,"

"Knitting for Uncle Sam" (No. 9396)

shows the fireplace of the hall, or kitchen, with a lengthy commentary starting on page 460. It is believed that the Nutting title is "Washington Trestle Table" (9308). This also is in the first edition.

Plate number 900-906, "Pine Settle, Carver Chairs, Roasting Jack, Candle Box," was also taken in the hall. The Nutting title is "Knitting for Uncle Sam" (9396), with an interesting commentary on page 592 as follows:

> Nos. 900-906. A room showing seventeenth and eighteenth century furniture. In the distance, against the plaster on the left, there is a tall iron candle stand. Over the fireplace hangs a bar on iron hooks. It was used to air ironed articles; sometimes a checkered apron, perhaps, was allowed to hang there as a sort of momentous warning to the youngsters. [This warning was: "If you don't behave yourself, I'll put you over my checkered apron and spank you," even if no checkered apron was being worn. Many times did I hear that warning.]
>
> On the right is a pine stool which is of a later period. Over the head of the grandfather, against the wall, there is a tin cylindrical candle box. The feet of the young lady are on a braided rug all made of corn husks, said to have been used in this form by the Indians. We doubt, however, whether the knowledge of braiding and rug making came to our ancestors from that source. No doubt some of their basket work was learned from the Indians.
>
> One sees in this picture the huge proportions of a summer beam, the great beam overhead at the left sustaining the floor timbers. The room is the kitchen of the Iron Works House, Saugus.

The title of this picture, "Knitting for Uncle Sam," was appropriate for the period in which it was taken — 1917. The United States had just entered the First World War, and the ladies were busy "knitting socks for soldiers," as well as pull-over sweaters and scarfs, which were distributed by the Red Cross to the volunteers and inductees.

The gentleman in the picture is Wallace Nutting's "Uncle Sam" Young and the lady is "a young lady who perhaps would not like her name mentioned," but this I doubt as I believe any young lady would be pleased to pose and have her name mentioned as having appeared in a setting such as this with "Uncle Sam." (With the attention he is giving her work, it would seem she is knitting for him.)

In 1922 Nutting published the first book of his "States Beautiful" series, *Vermont Beautiful,* and dedicated it to his wife: "To my wife whose company on Vermont roads and whose inspiration and good taste have made this and other work of mine possible."

This was somewhat of an elaborate book in that it had a regular index of text and also an index of pictures, as the pictures themselves were not titled, but in subsequent volumes of his "States Beautiful" series this index of pictures was discontinued and each picture was titled underneath. This seemed to me to be typical Wallace Nutting, start out with a flourish, and then tone down a bit.

This book also showed on page 295 the picture "An Old Fashioned Paradise," which was adapted by Nutting as more or less of a trademark, as it appeared on his billheads and stationery and was used on the title pages of his books and catalogs, and in some cases, advertising.

Nutting admired this old house: "The cottage was Vermont personafied. It was simple, honest, kindly, cozy, and independent." It was located in North Danville, Vermont.

A poem (purported to have been written by Nutting, but this I doubt) about the house and its association with the large elm trees appears on page 294:

> Cottage and elm began their day together;
> The one is breaking in the century's blast;
> Looming triumphant over wind and weather,
> The other shields its comrade to the last.
>
> Five generations in their home-nest here,
> Beneath the tree, have waxed to manhoods' might;
> Where still the boughs caress the ruin sere,
> The sun with lingering kiss still bids good-night.
>
> Grant us the gift of lengthening days,
> More winning and more mellow year by year;
> Give us the home-hearth with its cheering blaze,
> And crown us with such comradeship as here!

Seven years after that delightful day the old house had burned and the great elm had fallen in a storm, and this sequel was added:

> The flames have claimed the relics of my rhyme;
> The earth has called the elm back to her breast;
> I ponder in the ruins, past my prime,
> Upon the mysteries of change and rest.
>
> But other suns will raise up elms more fair,
> Beneath which better homes will rise;
> And stronger hearts will weave the life-thread there,
> And better minds will worthier rhymes devise.

I believe that this particular picture of the house was taken looking toward the front, but another one, more picturesque and more desirable to me was taken looking toward the back of the house. This shows the old elm in all its beauty "shielding" the cottage and its associated buildings. The title of this picture is "Two Centuries," and it is one of Nutting's earlier pictures, being copyrighted in 1901.

"An Old Fashioned Paradise" (No. 1843)   This photograph taken in Danville, Vt., served as the basis for the monogram used on Nutting's books, advertisements, and letterheads such as that below.

WALLACE NUTTING PICTURES
OLD AMERICA COMPANY
FORTY-SIX PARK STREET, FRAMINGHAM, MASSACHUSETTS

"Larkspur" (No. 6063)   Taken in Cheshire, England, this was one of Nutting's most popular photographs, having been sought after, according to his Photographic Art Secrets, *"by the hundred thousand."*

"The Coming Out of Rosa" (No. 2530) One of the most controversial of Nutting's photographs when it comes to describing its location and the identity of the subject, it was one of a series of pictures taken in the summer of 1911 of Elizabeth Sturdy Blackinton of North Attleboro, Mass. The lady is Mildred Codding, a friend of the Blackinton family who was chosen for the part of "mother" by Nutting because of her dark hair. This photograph, and its variations, were among Nutting's best sellers.

As *Vermont Beautiful* does contain many of his earliest and best pictures, with many interesting stories of this state, and the fact he dedicated this book to his wife Mariet, makes it my choice of his "States Beautiful" series.

After this, he continued on with *Massachusetts Beautiful, Connecticut Beautiful,* and *New Hampshire Beautiful* in 1923; then *Maine Beautiful,* which he dedicated to his father Albion, and *Pennsylvania Beautiful* in 1924. These were followed by *Ireland Beautiful* in 1925, *New York Beautiful* in 1927, *England Beautiful* in 1928, and finally *Virginia Beautiful* in 1930.

On the verso page of the revised edition of *Furniture of the Pilgrim Century* (1924), Nutting lists as "In Preparation," *Ohio Beautiful, Montana Beautiful* (with National Parks), *Washington Beautiful,* and *Florida Beautiful.* Then in *Furniture Treasury,* volume I (1928), he also repeats *Florida Beautiful* and lists *New Jersey Beautiful* and *California Beautiful* in two volumes, as well as *Mohonk and the Smileys.* In volume III of *Furniture Treasury* (1933), he continues to list *California Beautiful* "to issue possibly 1935," and *Florida Beautiful* "to issue perhaps in 1934."

I have never seen any evidence that any of the above books were done, or in preparation, except *Florida Beautiful,* of which 22 typewritten pages were found in the museum at Framingham Library among the papers of Alan Carter, who at one time was researching Nutting. Nutting did take pictures in the above-named states, some of which I have and some are listed in his catalogs.

Again, I have seen no evidence that *Mohonk and the Smileys* was published. Mohonk was a summer resort on Lake Mohonk at New Platz, New York, operated by the Smiley Brothers since long before the turn of the century.

No doubt that the Nuttings and the Smileys were friends, and that this was one of their favorite haunts, but Nutting does not mention the Smileys or Mohonk in his *Biography,* and this seems strange to me, unless they had a "falling out" prior to his *Biography,* but on page 86 of *New York Beautiful,* first edition, he comments as follows:

> Mohonk Lake is not second in beauty and striking features to any natural object in the east. It has happily been preserved, with Lake Minnewaska, its neighbor, to quiet, and dignity. The combined drives on the environs of these lakes approach one hundred miles. They are laid, but with the express idea of preserving the majesty of the great cliffs and of bringing them into the best perspective. They are a perpetual monument to Albert Smiley and those related to him, who have done so much to unveil the noblest of our scenery.

In the interim of the foregoing publications he supposedly published his *Birthday Book* in 1924, but again I have never seen a copy of it, or know of anyone who has a copy, and have not found any mention of it in any of his writings. It could have been put together by someone else.

It listed the months of the year from January to December, depicting each month with a picture suitable for the season, using both interior and exterior prints, and also contained the poem "The House by the Side of the Road" by Sam Walter Foss, who was at one time head of a library in Somerville, Massachusetts. Some of these prints are shown in his "States Beautiful" books.

Also in 1924 he published the first edition of *The Clock Book,* showing 250 pictures of many types of clocks of American and foreign manufacture, with the description of the illustrations in a separate chapter. Nutting also lists the names of the American and foreign clockmakers and the dates when the maker flourished. The second edition of this work was done in 1935.

In 1927 he continued on with *Photographic Art Secrets,* first edition, published by Dodd Mead Co. of New York; the second edition came out in 1931. In this work he asks the question, "Is Photography an Art?," and answers with "most of it is not," and elaborates on the use of equipment, the compositions of the pictures and their selection, the processes of developing and printing, and locations of his plates, 105 of which he shows and comments on.

He refers to the word "photographer" as being "a cameraist," and he states, "pardon the new word," which he no doubt coined. He considered himself to be a "cameraist." At one time I loaned this book to a professional photographer and he said that "the man was a genius" and he learned a great deal from it.

In 1930 a book entitled *Pathways of the Puritans* was compiled by Mrs. N. F. Bell for the Commonwealth of Massachusetts for the celebration of the tercentenary of the founding of the Massachusetts Bay Colony, and was published by Wallace Nutting's Old America Co., for which he supplied 33 of his own pictures of historic houses erected prior to the year 1750, showing interior or exterior, and furnished the information concerning them. This work was done in three editions, but in the acknowledgements Wallace Nutting's name was not found in any edition, but "Courtesy Wallace Nutting" followed the title of the pictures.

In 1936 *Wallace Nutting's Biography* was published by Old America Co. "Why should that fellow presume to write an autobiography?" He explained that "these were hard times and I have sold it [the biography]." Also he assumed that after he realized that people were reading his "States Beautiful" books, they might be interested in a biography. As he had received many requests for material from school children who had been assigned the task of writing a sketch of his life, he thought that the biography was the answer, and would "squelch the inquiries."

It seems he must have thought of his life as an "Adventure," as some of the chapters are titled "Adventures of . . ." and "Adventures in . . ." such as " Adventures of Youth," "Adventures in Picture Making," and "Adventures in the Search of Beauty." The latter was used under the title of "The Quest of Beauty" by him at the commencement exercises of Washington and Jefferson College on June 8, 1935, where he was honored with the degree of Doctor of Humanities. There were other "Adventures" in matrimony, preaching, farming, travel, antiques, reproductions, old houses, foreign art, lecturing, labor, and publishing. There is also a chapter on "Harmony in Life" in which he explains his conclusion on the subject. It also contains a "Resume" of his life and a chapter titled "Guide Posts (from a Private Diary)," and it is assumed that it was his diary, as he was known to have kept one. It contains proverbs on the different views of life and living.

He states in his "Resume" that he "wrote some twelve hundred definitions on furniture and iron, as associate editor of *Webster's New International Dictionary,* 1933." On checking this volume, nothing was found to indicate he was an "associate editor" and there were no associate editors named under the editorial staff. He was one of 147 "Special Editors" whose portraits were shown, and he was number 11, "Wallace Nutting, Furniture." Again this indicates his self-centered and egotistical manner.

In the third volume of *Furniture Treasury* under "Glossary" he wrote: "The author had the honor to revise and add to twelve hundred terms relating to furniture and hardware for a new edition of an unabridged dictionary, but it seems convenient to include those terms here." In checking some of those terms (selected at random from the "Glossary") against the same words as found in an early dictionary, and one after 1933, the definitions are the same, or the words have been compounded or hyphenated by Nutting, to suit the application to furniture or hardware.

Adventures in Old Houses

In January 1915 Nutting, with his architect Charles Henry Dean, inspected the Iron Works House at Saugus and both decided that it was well worth saving and restoring. He purchased the house, at that time known as the "Old Iron Works House," on March 2, 1915, from George Niven. It had been greatly changed from its original version as built in the 1640s, as it had been converted into a tenement house, as two entrances are shown on the east end and a long porch had been added to the front, as can be seen in a picture taken about 1900.

"Broadhearth, The Iron Works House," Saugus, Mass., shortly after the completion of its restoration by Nutting in 1916. The original barn still stands behind the house to the right; it would shortly be replaced by a shop for Nutting's blacksmith and caretaker, Edward Guy.

This was the first of the very old houses which Wallace Nutting restored (1916), and it was his oldest exhibition house. In late 1917 he had changed ownership from Wallace Nutting of Framingham to Wallace Nutting Incorporated. He called this house "Broadhearth, The Iron Works House," and wrote an interesting and descriptive brochure on the construction, the interior of the rooms and fireplaces, and the antique furnishings displayed.

The house is one of the very few in America where posts were cut off at the top of the first story and beams were run out a foot and a half beyond the posts, as a foundation for a second story. This type of construction was sometimes referred to as an "overhang house." Also found was evidence that there had been a "projecting porch," and projecting downwards from the overhang were drops of quaint design.

The study of the chimney of this house showed a great formation with opposite fireplaces in the fireroom, or kitchen, and the parlor. These fireplaces were nearly 10 feet across and 3½ feet deep. At a later time a leanto was added with a large fireplace which carried its flue up a slant to meet the central chimney stack, and this formed a T-shaped top.

A fireplace of this era would have a cast iron slab called a fireback to protect the back of the fireplace, because the continued heat would finally destroy the brick in the back, unless thus protected. The bottom of the fireplace was made of brick tile seven to eight inches square, extending into the room to act as a hearth.

Another feature of the original house was the size of the rooms, both on the first and second floors, with two fireplaces on the second floor.

The ell on the west side, although not part of the original house, is quite old, and this was changed architecturally to conform to the original house, and here is where the caretaker and blacksmith, Edward Guy, lived with his family. He was hired to reproduce 17th and 18th century ironwork for Nutting.

His blacksmith shop or forge was located behind the house, and this is the shop Guy owned in Newburyport, where he conducted his business prior to going to Saugus. The shop was dismantled, moved by rail to Saugus, and carted to the present site by a team of horses, and erected as it was until recently remodeled. Here Guy, with his son Edward L. (Les) Guy and other blacksmiths, hammered out reproductions of old iron hardware and hand-made nails.

Quite sometime after the Wallace Nutting period of ownership this shop was used to display artifacts of the original iron works dug up during the restoration period from 1948 to 1954, both large and small, including parts of the sluiceways and old waterwheels as well as small tools. On the original wood floor could be seen the burn marks of hot iron, reminiscent of the work that went on there. This was one of my favorite spots when visiting the Iron Works before the modernization.

This shop has been turned into a more modern museum showing a model of the iron works, as well as modern display cases, showing smaller artifacts, with explanations. The outside appearance of this shop was greatly changed during the modernization. Frankly, I prefer the old shop as it was during and after the Nutting period.

At the east end of the museum today stands a sweet cherry tree, still bearing fruit, planted there by Les Guy and his brother George when they were kids. George was lost at sea in a storm off the coast of Labrador while on a training cruise as a Merchant Marine cadet. Les also built the leanto, or porch, against the ell on the north side of the main house when he was 15 years old, and it is still there today.

Wallace Nutting produced at least 37 hand-colored pictures of the interior of the Iron Works House. Les Guy's sister Elizabeth posed in some of them. His favorite model was Miss Daisy Ryder, a pretty blonde girl, who also posed in pictures of other houses.

One winter when Mrs. Nutting was staying in California, Wallace slept at the Iron Works House in the parlor chamber, he at one end and Les Guy at the other end, as Nutting did not want to be in the room alone.

At one time Wallace had intentions of building a house in Saugus, near the iron works, to avoid long treks from Framingham Center, but Mrs. Nutting frowned upon this, and refused to leave the Framingham home, so the idea was abandoned.

Before World War I, in 1917, Nutting bought the old Scott Mill in Saugus, along with some tenement houses, which adjoined the old iron works property. The mill was run by water power, but soon after Nutting had the old waterwheel dismantled and converted to all-electric power, and, as has been mentioned before, here is where he published his first book, *American Windsors,* and also continued the picture business, employing many local girls as colorists.

Adventures in Reproductions

It was also at the Scott Mill that he started the reproduction of Early American furniture in 1917, and he states, "The reproduction of furniture I indulged in partly to find out how the old was made." Some of his staff would take the original piece of furniture apart, make sketches, and proceed to make the copy.

He also had other reasons for making the reproductions. When he was unsuccessful in finding authentic furniture for his restored colonial homes, he proceeded to supply his own copies. The reproductions also allowed people who could not pay collector's prices, but who wanted to furnish their houses nostalgically, to own "old furniture," "and to keep faith with the public." He was at one time accused of selling the reproductions as antiques, but this was not true.

His first furniture reproductions were marked with an elaborate white-and-green label 5½ inches by 8 inches, listing items of "hand work" furniture and "wrought-iron colonial, and early English house hardware in latches, hinges, candlesticks, scones. . . ." In reference to "scones," this word was misspelled; the correct spelling of course would be "sconces." A scone is a thin cake made of barley or wheat meal, of Scottish origin (pronounced "skon"). A sconce is a hanging or projecting candlestick. It would be rather difficult to chew on a wrought iron "scone." I believe the printer must have made the error in spelling as Nutting's writing is rather difficult to decipher, as I have found out.

No. 303. Small Braced Bow-back, Rhode Island Leg

This dainty light chair was for a lady, as the seat is smaller than the average. This variant of the leg turning was popular in Rhode Island.

From a catalog published by Wallace Nutting, Inc., Saugus Center, Mass., around 1918.

Nutting operated at the Scott Mill until early 1920, when he sold the Old Iron Works House to Charles F. Cooney, an antique dealer, who used the home to display his own furniture. Nutting then moved his picture and furniture business to Ashland, Massachusetts, purchasing an old canning factory there, as it had the facility of a spur track where he could receive his raw materials and ship out his finished products by rail. He continued to use the paper labels modified to a great extent from the lavish first label.

At this time he stated the business owed $120,000 in the enlarged Ashland Studio. The picture business was actually supporting the furniture business, which was a losing venture. This was unknown to Mrs. Nutting at the time; not until after Wallace's death did she become aware of it.

He continued on here until 1922, when, due to ill health, he retired and sold all business interests with the right to use the name "Wallace Nutting," but being dissatisfied with the conduct of the business and the poor quality of the work produced, being branded in script "Wallace Nutting," he bought back all stock and rights in 1924. In order to do this, he sold his own personal collection of Pilgrim furniture to J. P. Morgan, who, in turn, donated the collection to the Wadsworth Atheneum in Hartford, Connecticut, where it can be seen on display today.

I have attended auctions where the script mark was referred to as being an "original Wallace Nutting signed piece" and have also seen them displayed in antique shops as such. The signature in the script brand was not Wallace Nutting's own signature but was done by one of his employees, and appeared a great many times in Nutting's own picture and furniture advertisements while at the Ashland Studio. It was never used by him as a mark on his furniture produced in Ashland, but was copied and used by the people who bought the business in 1922.

In 1925 he purchased the old straw shop at 46 Park Street, Framingham (then called South Framingham), and claims he spent $57,000 preparing for the reestablishment of his picture and furniture business as "Wallace Nutting Furniture, Inc.," and issued several catalogs pertaining to furniture, and explicitly said, "I will not be responsible for a script letter formerly used as a mark." He also showed a copy of the brand "WALLACE NUTTING" done in block letters, and stated, "This brand must appear on all my furniture." In some cases a label appeared with the brand, being smaller than his earlier labels.

In 1925 the Nuttings made a third journey abroad, mainly to England and Ireland, "for picture making for my colored pictures and books." On the return trip they met on the ship a young effeminate and shy Irish lad from Dublin, Ernest John Donnelly, of whom Nutting said, "He is a genius in sketching and criticism and accounting," and he was hired by Nutting to work at the studio at 46 Park Street, Framingham.

"Ernest John," as he was affectionately called by his co-workers, performed many tasks for Nutting, but his principal job was making "pentype sketches" of old houses, including some interiors showing the fireplaces and period furniture. These were taken from photographs done by Nutting, many of which are to be found in his "States Beautiful" books and his furniture books, more especially volume III of *Furniture Treasury,* but here Nutting over-credits Donnelly when he says he "made all sketches for Volume III."

Another contributor of sketches to this volume was Kenneth Wood of Framingham, who worked for Nutting during his spare time and summer

Christmas Greetings from Nuttingholme

vacations while attending Massachusetts Institute of Technology as an architectural student. He did the decorative and shell sketches as used on furniture, as well as furniture parts. Nutting also credits a Mr. J. S. Crytzer for the measured drawings shown in this volume.

Other promotions by Donnelly were the pentypes. "The name and the theme are something new." These consisted of black-and-white silhouettes, Mother's Day cards, note cards, and Christmas cards; a popular one of the

One of the pentype silhouettes done for
Nutting by Ernest John Donnelly.

latter shows Mr. and Mrs. Nutting sitting at a table writing cards, the title, "Christmas Greetings from Nuttingholme," done in Old English lettering. This was their own personal Christmas card. These sketches were usually reproduced by the use of zinc plates for printing in his portfolio, and Nutting's books and advertisements.

In 1929 Nutting was contacted by the D.A.R. Museum in Washington, D.C., in regard to designing a room, and furnishing the plan and pine panelling, etc., to match the 1770 chimney breast removed from an old house in Haverhill, New Hampshire, and to be installed in the "New Hampshire Children's Attic," a commemorative room in Memorial Continental Hall at the museum. Nutting thought of it as a colonial children's bedroom, and since then it has become an area for a large collection of 19th century toys and children's furniture.

Nutting originally made one plan for the room, which was rejected. He submitted the second and third which were also rejected as being too ornate, and finally his first plan was accepted and carried out.

The original measurements made in early 1930 by Nutting were lost or mislaid, and Donnelly, acting as secretary, requested new measurements from the Building Committee which were received, and "pieces of wood"

The New Hampshire Children's Attic in the D.A.R. Museum in Washington as it appeared in 1934, shortly after completion.

BUCKINGHAM STUDIO, COURTESY D.A.R. MUSEUM

were sent by express, and the balance of the material was sent by truck, and there is no doubt that Donnelly handled the entire project for Nutting.

Nutting furnished the pine panelling to match the chimney breast, furnished two corner cupboards for $1,000, made a cabinet and wooden radiator masks, and made a drawing for a chandelier for the room, which was accepted and the museum had it made. Nutting also donated a settee. This room is maintained by the D.A.R. of New Hampshire.

Sharing the responsibilities of conducting the business with Donnelly for Nutting at 46 Park Street was Esther Svenson, who worked previously at the Framingham Center Studio, now acting as head colorist and also "a right hand man" for Nutting. Her name is found in Nutting's list of "First Line Friends" as being in his employ at the time for 24 years.

Nutting continued on with his lectures and lantern slide shows of his pictures and furniture, mainly as an advertising promotion. Del Goding, his chauffeur while at Saugus, went with him on one trip to Illinois or somewhere in the Mid-West, and recalled that Nutting got $60 for a lecture and chuckled about it. "What do you know about that?" Nutting said. "I got $60 for advertising my own material." That is the way Nutting looked at things.

It was while at 46 Park Street that he discovered that his pictures were being reproduced and sold at a cheap price. Some of these reproductions were purchased and taken back to the office and shown to Nutting, who became very upset and exclaimed, "Why, they are pirates!" and told Donnelly to call his lawyer, and later a lawsuit followed.

These pictures were being reproduced by a printing method, not hand colored, sometimes using Nutting's own titles, but unsigned, and showing no copyright of Nutting's. They were done in various sizes, with and without a black or dark brown border. Some have been found with "M&B, Inc." on the lower left corner of the picture, or a 14000 series number, such as "No. 14609 PRINTED IN U.S.A.," on the lower left-hand corner of the mount. Morris and Bendien, Inc., a New York concern, was responsible for some "pirated" pictures, but is it not definitely known who did the "14000" pictures.

Some reproductions have been found with a green label in the shape of a leaf on the back of the dust cover as "Nature Views — Reproductions from the Originals by Nutting. Borin Art Products Corp., Chicago."

A pirated print or picture has been found with "©M&B INC." on the front of it, and on the back of the dust cover a round stamped-on label of Borin Art Products was found, so it would appear that Borin was framing reproductions from Nutting's originals for Morris and Bendien in some cases.

NUTTING LABELS

An all hand colored print.
Signature protected by law.
No. *E-1/2*

WALLACE NUTTING

Authentic Wallace Nutting
Process Pictures must bear
this Label. All others are
unauthorized.

**WALLACE NUTTING
FURNITURE**

STYLE AND STRENGTH

Table No.
All Hand Turned
All Maple
Amber Finish
Mortised and Pinned
Square Pegs
In Round Holes.
Supremacy
In Reproductions.
A Good Name Is Better
Than Great Riches
Name Burned In

*The label at left was a tag tied on-
to Nutting's furniture reproductions. The others appeared on the
dust covers of his photographs.*

This subject is
copyrighted. Original features
added by hand. All negatives
made by me are owned by me.
Use of my name is unauthorized. All rights reserved.
No. *D-3491*

WALLACE NUTTING

Leaf-shaped label, used by Borin Art Products on the pirated copies of Nutting's pictures.

A copyright on a Nutting picture protected it from being reproduced for a certain number of years only. Some of the pictures that were pirated were copyrighted by Nutting between 1900 and 1919, prior to the Morris and Bendien era, which occurred after 1925.

The lawsuit was settled to the extent that Nutting's pictures which were in a copyright status could not be reproduced, and/or his own original titles could not be used. The so-called "pirated" prints or pictures finally disappeared from the market. They are considered a collector's item by many today.

I firmly believe that this is when, later on, Nutting, or someone in his employ, got the idea to come out with his "Authentic Process Pictures," which occurred in the 1930s. He chose eight of his subjects for this first venture, six taken in England and Ireland and two in the Berkshires in Massachusetts. They were done in one size only, approximately 15 by 12 inches. There were five horizontals and three verticals. On the lower left front can be seen the copyright, "©WALLACE NUTTING." Some were framed close, which would hide the copyright, and others mounted and framed, showing a good margin.

In 1942, the year after Nutting's death, four more subjects were added, all taken in New Hampshire, and all horizontals. On the front of these on the lower right-hand bottom can be seen "COPYRIGHT 1942 WALLACE NUTTING."

As these were printed, they can be easily distinguished from a hand-colored photograph by using a magnifying glass, which will show tiny dots and/or a crosshatching effect. These pictures when mounted and framed were never signed with Nutting's name, and only the title appeared, always on the right-hand side under the picture on the mount.

A glued label was applied to the dust cover after framing to identify it as "A Wallace Nutting Process Picture," giving the title and Nutting number, "By Wallace Nutting." Another read as follows: "Authentic Wallace Nutting Process Pictures must bear this label. All others are unauthorized. No. — —."

These Process Pictures are being falsely advertised as "Wallace Nutting Hand Colored Photographs," and in some cases sold at a premium price. There are many of them available today, unmounted and unframed, for a very small cost. They did not sell too well for the Nutting Company and production of these ceased. They are also a desirable collector's item.

During the period before, or while at 46 Park Street, Nutting established his "Ten Construction Commandments" to "insure individuality and make men while making furniture":

1. *All work to be of the best quality.*
2. *If the old method is best, use it.*
3. *If the work can be done better by hand, do it that way.*
4. *Use long and large mortises, and large square white oak pins.*
5. *Make all joined work to fit perfectly, using draw bore where it is better.*
6. *Match the color where two pieces come together.*
7. *Follow the sample strictly. Take no liberties.*
8. *The hand and the mouth do not work effectively at the same time.*
9. *Keep busy, do your best, and no fault will be found.*
10. *Let nothing leave your hands until you are proud of the work.*

He furnished several invoices of furniture for the restoration of Williamsburg, Virginia, partly for the Raleigh Tavern, the House of Burgesses, and the vestibule of William and Mary College.

Evidently his own "Construction Commandments" were not adherred to on one invoice of chairs, as they were rejected by Williamsburg and returned to him as unsatisfactory. He eventually replaced them with a new invoice, rather than try to correct the original pieces, which no doubt were disposed of satisfactorily to him.

He also furnished complete sets of office furniture reproductions for banks and other business establishments. Included in this would be superbly hooked carpets made under the personal supervison of Mrs. Nutting, who imported a special broadloom burlap requiring no seaming, supervised the dyeing of the yarn, drew the patterns, and actually participated in the hooking of the carpets and rugs. All were usually signed by Mrs. Nutting's initials. There were six known carpets made from her patterns, namely the "Rose," "Heart," "Peacock," "Medallion," "Briar," and "Bluebell and Rose" carpets, the smallest of the six being 8 feet 9 inches by 7 feet. The largest was 14 feet by 12 feet.

In 1934 there was a lady employed at 46 Park Street who did hand-weaving of runners, scarfs, table sets, and towels, etc. She did this on her own exclusive of the Nuttings, although the articles were tagged as being done at the Wallace Nutting Studio "by Mary Jones Smith." Nutting no doubt accepted this as an asset to his business to enhance his sales of furniture.

"Heart" rug pattern by Mrs. Mariet Nutting. This represents a little over half of a rug measuring 12 feet 5 inches by 10 feet.

As the business continued on in the late 1930s, Nutting depended more and more on Ernest John Donnelly and Esther Svenson and at times did not come to the studio regularly, due to failing health, and when he did come he only spent a few hours.

As sales had fallen off greatly in all branches of the business, Donnelly informed Nutting that there was a financial difficulty and Nutting's reply was, "Providence will provide." But "Providence" did not provide and practically everyone was laid off.

Nutting stated that "it is really old age that compels me to quit, getting tired and no longer able to cope with reversing problems in the business." He had at this time also said he was going to "close out" the furniture business.

This was the era of the presidential election of 1940, and although Wendell Wilkie was defeated by Franklin Roosevelt, Nutting stated in a letter to his life-long friend Fred Snow, "Of the millions subsidized by the dictator [meaning Roosevelt], many must have disputed his right, since a change of 2,000,000 would have given Wilkie the election." Wilkie had received 44 percent of the popular vote, the greatest ever received by a defeated candidate up to that time.

Nutting's visits to the studio became less frequent as the spring of 1941 progressed, and his last visit was a few days before he died on July 19, 1941, of "chronic cardiac degeneration" according to official records at Framingham Town Hall, although it has been written that he died of cancer. In checking medical and funeral director's records no reference to cancer could be found.

He was laid to rest on July 21, 1941, in the Mount Pleasant Cemetery, Augusta, Maine, where his mother Eliza, his sister Edith, and wife Mariet also lie. His father, as noted previously, is buried in the Arlington National Cemetery.

In 1930 the Associated Press prepared a "condensed sketch" (Sketch 1786) on "Wallace Nutting ... Antiquarian." It was prefaced with a note to editors: "The following biographical sketch of Wallace Nutting is for use PRIMARILY IN EVENT OF HIS DEATH. The material, but not the actual text, may be used in connection with current news events." It started out with one of his favorite sayings, "I never learned to live until I was fifty," and went on to give an outline of his career. This "condensed sketch" was followed by an additional article about his pastorates, picture making, antiques, tribulations, and publishing of "treatises on antiques."

After the death of Nutting, Mrs. Nutting with the able assistance of Donnelly and Miss Svenson carried on the business until her death in August 1944 at the age of 90 years.

In April 1942 she had made her "last will" leaving to Donnelly and Miss Svenson the picture business, "and all the plates, stock, and materials . . . including the good will and the use of the name Wallace Nutting . . . only so long as . . . one of them shall continue personally to carry on or to control . . . said business." This also included the publishing business known as Old America Co.

A cash bequest of $1,000 was left John Kelly "in recognition of faithful service for over twenty years." Other cash bequests of $1,000 and $500 were left to nieces and nephews, designated in some cases "to be used in the education of their children."

The remainder of the estate of "whatever name and nature" was bequeathed to Berea College of Berea, Kentucky, a pet charity of the Nuttings. It was an institution dedicated to serving the Appalachian youth, with a no-tuition policy. Nutting had delivered the commencement address there in 1900.

This bequest included the furniture business and building at 46 Park Street, Framingham, which not long after was sold by the college to a concern in Drexel, Burke County, North Carolina. It then became known as "Wallace Nutting Furniture, Inc., a Delaware Corporation, with a principal place of business at Framingham, Mass." (It was generally known as "The Drexel Co.") As far as is known, it never did anything with the furniture business, and it was abandoned by it as being too costly.

Also included in this bequest to Berea was Nuttingholme, the home of the Nuttings in Framingham Center. This property was later acquired by the First Parish Unitarian Universalist Church to be developed into a community and church center. It had been used as a church school and parsonage since 1945, and was finally torn down in February 1964 to make way for a parking lot and Scott Hall, a church-associated building.

In October 1945 Donnelly sold his interest in the picture and publishing business to Esther Svenson, to take effect on January 1, 1946, and she was to employ him until April 1, 1946, at $25 a week. He later went to work for a Boston concern, making silhouettes and small pictures, but this venture not being fruitful, he moved to Philadelphia and associated himself with an antique dealer, and continued there for quite some time. He returned to his native Ireland in 1970, and died there in 1973. He never married.

In an agreement made in November 1945 between the "Delaware Corporation" and Esther Svenson, the corporation agreed to sell her the property at 46 Park Street, to be conveyed on or before May 1, 1946.

It seems coincidental that this transaction was consummated after Donnelly had agreed to sell his interests in the business to Miss Svenson, and one might speculate that there had been friction between Donnelly and Svenson. This was not the case, however, and they corresponded periodically until the time of her death.

After the acquisition of the property, Miss Svenson conducted the business in a small way for about six years. It was known as "Wallace Nutting Pictures, Old America Company, Esther R. Svenson, Owner and Manager."

This building also had other tenants at this time, the C. W. Hansen Co., a local furniture company not associated in any way with the Nutting enterprises, and Webb Supply, a plumbing supply house.

In August 1952 Miss Svenson sold the property only to R. W. Patten of Framingham Center, as she wanted to continue the business in smaller quarters, which she decided to do at her home, 587 Union Avenue, Framingham. Here she did some coloring and continued to fill orders for about two years, or as long as the supply of pictures and books lasted.

She entered a local nursing home in 1971, and at that time gave much material pertinent to Nutting to the Framingham Center Library. She had also given orders to have the glass negatives destroyed, and she was no doubt carrying out the wishes of Mrs. Nutting, who feared that the quality of work might not be up to the Nutting standard if done by someone else.

As evidenced today, much of it was either overlooked or salvaged from the dump at the time, as many of the glass negatives and other unusual memorabilia are owned by collectors. Miss Svenson died on December 8, 1972, at the age of 83. She was unmarried. She had been associated with the Nutting enterprises for about 40 years.

The saga of Wallace Nutting did not end here, as in October 1973 the "Wallace Nutting Collectors Club" was started by Mrs. Justine Monro of New Jersey, with the able assistance of her husband George. It is comprised of people, most of whom are private collectors, "having an interest in learning more about Wallace Nutting; the man and his works," and dedicated to preservation of his achievements. Much has been learned about this man through the contributions of these members.

In 1983 the National Park Service recognized Nutting's role in the early historic preservation movement when it began a program to restore the exterior of the Iron Works House at Saugus to its 1917 appearance. In addition, the exhibit plan for the house calls for the west chamber to be furnished as Nutting depicted it in his photograph "Affectionately Yours" (No. 9324). It will thus serve as a permanent monument to his memory.

Perhaps it would be appropriate to repeat a citation given to Wallace Nutting by Washington and Jefferson College shortly after he gave the commencement address there in 1935. This citation is not likely to be surpassed by any later estimate of the lifework of this famous man:

> We honor you as one who has devoted a great life to the quest for beauty and who, finding beauty, has revealed it to the world with peculiar force. Called to the ministry of the church, your quest led you to a beautiful God as the redeeming and sublimating element in a world otherwise red in tooth and claw. Health frustration limiting your ministry, you sought beauty still, and found it in little gardens, in homes built by humble hands who knew not their own artistry, in hand-woven rugs where imprisoned souls had found creative release, in furniture where imperishable values of line and form flowed from the workmanship of pioneers. These elements of line, form and color which our preoccupied generation would have missed and even destroyed, you discovered, preserved and revealed. Your pictures in literally millions of homes, your reproductions of furniture, your books and your ceaseless quest for and advocacy of beauty have together constituted an appreciable element in our culture and civilization.

SOURCES

Many articles have been written about Wallace Nutting, portions of which contain many distorted facts, and erroneous statements, and it is hoped that this booklet in part might tend to shed a different light on this man and his accomplishments.

Much of the information used in the compilation of this booklet came from Nutting's own writings, both published and unpublished. Most of his "States Beautiful" books are currently available in reprint editions, as are his works on furniture. It is a tribute to his work that they are still in demand after a half century.

The main collection of Nutting material is to be found at the library in Framingham Center, Mass. The Wadsworth Atheneum in Hartford, Ct., has his collection of antique furniture, while the library of the Society for the Preservation of New England Antiquities in Boston has a collection of Nutting photographs.

Former employees of Nutting and the other individuals mentioned in the acknowledgements provided me with their recollections, helping to fill in and give color to his personality.

The published literature on Nutting is small, and is mostly in the form of articles. One of the earliest of these is Marion T. Colley's "I Never Learned to Live Until I Was Fifty," *American Magazine*, January 1927, which includes quotations from interviews with Nutting. Other articles include Helen Comstock, "Wallace Nutting and the *Furniture Treasury* in Retrospect," *Antiques*, Nov. 1961; Henry P. Maynard, "The Wadsworth Atheneum and Wallace Nutting," *The Connecticut Antiquarian*, December 1961; and "The Nutting Collection," *Colonial Homes*, May-June 1982.

John Freeman's essay, "The Art-Crafts Ideology or Wallace Nutting's Colonial Revival," appeared as an introduction to the American Life Foundation & Study Institute's 1969 reprint of Nutting's *Checklist of Early American Reproductions*. Professor William L. Dulaney of Pennsylvania State University has had articles on Nutting in *Americana* for July-Aug. 1978 and *Fine Woodworking* for Mar.-Apr. 1983, and in Winterthur Portfolio No. 13, *American Furniture and Its Makers* (1979). Charles B. Hosmer, Jr., discusses Nutting's role in the early historic preservation movement, with emphasis on the Wentworth-Gardener House in Portsmouth, N.H., in his *Presence of the Past* (1965).

Two catalogs deserve mention here. The first, prepared by Parke-Bernet Galleries of New York in 1941, *Fine Early American Furniture* (Sale No. 299), provides descriptions of the furniture left by Nutting as part of his estate. The second, *Wallace Nutting Pictures* (1980), compiled and published by Willis B. White, Jr., provides a catalog of Nutting titles and a brief sketch of his career.

While none of these works, as well as the numerous brief pieces which have appeared in other magazines over the years, are totally free from error, they were a good starting point for a study of this highly complex individual.

ACKNOWLEDGEMENTS

The preparation of a booklet such as this involves many people. Mary Borg convinced me to undertake this project, translated my handwriting into typescript, and graciously consented to provide the "About the Author" sketch for the booklet. Steve Carlson and Dick Provenzano, as well as Doris Felch, provided constant encouragement. Steve did the bulk of the copyediting of the manuscript and also typed the final copy.

Deserving special thanks are those individuals who took the time to share with me their recollections of Wallace Nutting or otherwise help me in this endeavor: Les Guy, Del and Lowell Goding, Everett Nutting, Margaret Hennessey, Elizabeth (Guy) Cota, Ruth (Harris) Young, Kenneth Wood, Florence McCarrier, Beatrice Julien, Florence Day, Joel Huston Dodge, Mabel B. Lovejoy, Tom and Abby Griffin, Alsina (Allaire) Carter, Mr. and Mrs. Louis Husson, Mr. and Mrs. John Blackinton, Earl Hills, Naomi Murray, Ruth (Flood) Frazier, Bob Nelson, Marie Sladen and her neice Mrs. Joshua Loring, Dorothy Rothe of the Malden (Mass.) Public Library, Isabel (Foss) Ballou, John Whelton, Robert E. McLaughlin, William Bowers, Julia Esty, Sarah Dunn, Gertrude Brown, Alan Carter, and Kenneth Baker.

Mrs. Hilda Cushing, sister of Esther Svenson, also provided valuable information and extended many courtesies to me. Laura Moxon and Beatrice Turner, who worked together at the library at Framingham Center, facilitated my research into the Nutting collection there.

Other institutions which have provided material include the Congregational Library of Boston; the Groton (Mass.) Public Library; the D.A.R. Museum of Washington, D.C.; the United Church of Christ, Minneapolis, Minn.; the Ramsay County Historical Society, St. Paul, Minn.; the Minnesota Historical Society; the Harvard University Library; the First Parish Church, Framingham, Mass.; the Metropolitan Museum of Art, New York; the Wadsworth Atheneum, Hartford, Ct.; Berea College, Berea, Ky.; and the Old Military Branch of the National Archives, Washington, D.C.

I am also grateful to the assistance provided by Joyce Barendsen, who is currently working on a booklet on Nutting's days at Southbury, Ct., and to Cynthia Pollack of the Saugus Iron Works for making available Orville Carroll's fine architectural study of the Iron Works House.

This work is also indebted to the members of the Wallace Nutting Collectors Club and especially Justine and George Monro and the many individuals who have, through their published articles or letters, spurred me to dig deeper into the Wallace Nutting story. They are too numerous to list here, and I wish also to apologize to others who may have helped me who have gone nameless here.

Finally, in an indirect way, it was Wallace Nutting himself who first interested me in him. Around the year 1912 he came to my grandmother's house in Natick at least a half dozen times when I was there. He was interested in buying some of the antiques in the house, in par-

"Floating Lilies" (No. 3418) The grandfather clock to the right in this picture taken in the Farwell House in Natick was bought by Nutting from the author's grandmother.

ticular a large grandfather clock. Nutting had a reputation of not liking children, so I wasn't noticed; he was interested in the clock. He sort of pestered my grandmother to sell it, and eventually she did for $300. Many years later, when I saw the clock in one of his photographs, it reminded me of this incident and sparked my interest in finding out more about this man.

ABOUT THE AUTHOR

The material from which this booklet is written has been carefully documented by the author, Louis MacKeil. He was not content to accept "facts" as gathered by others. For many years Louis searched for truths. He corresponded with people who knew Nutting, and followed up on known sources of information, traveled great distances when necessary, sometimes just to copy a paper, and kept volumes of notes. The compilation of records derived from the notes has yielded a fascinating personal portrait of Wallace Nutting.

Nutting's unending quest for beauty and the ways in which he imparted the knowledge he wished to share with his followers is artistically drawn by MacKeil. The reader is allowed to enjoy inside humor, learn about the difficulties encountered by Nutting employees, follow the steps which led to the many moves and ventures undertaken, and then left to draw his own conclusions as to the character of this controversial man.

Louis MacKeil, a down-to-earth individual, interprets his material with good old fashion horse sense and Yankee ingenuity. There is nothing in this booklet which has been contrived out of imagination for dramatic purposes.

Nutting is known to have made the following request: "I beg to assure everybody concerned that I am too old to entertain hard feelings, though some persons have given me cause. I have nothing but hope for all men, among whom, as an object of hope, I would like to be included." Author MacKeil's work yields a finished product which is one step beyond any currently available and does much to fulfill Nutting's request.

MARY L. BORG, President
The Saugus Historical Society, Inc.

SAUGUS HISTORICAL SOCIETY BOOKLET SERIES

Edited by Stephen P. Carlson

No. 1. All Aboard! Public Transit in Saugus
by Stephen P. Carlson

No. 2. Wallace Nutting
by Louis M. MacKeil

No. 3. Pirates' Glen & Dungeon Rock
by Richard G. Provenzano

No. 4. Saugus Memories: A Selection of Postcard Views
*by Stephen P. Carlson, Edward W. Patterson, Jr.,
Richard G. Provenzano*